A Guide for Teachers
PREVENTING
PHYSICAL PROBLEMS
IN
VIOLIN
PLAYING

Vic Pomer

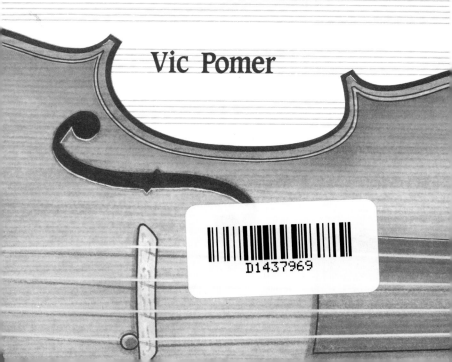

"I believe this valuable handbook of preventive possible problems for beginners, is the natural and inevitable outcome of a colleague-teacher as observant and experienced as Mr. Pomer. I sincerely hope it will guide and positively assist many instructors in the formative and important years of violin teaching."

Steven Staryk
Professor of Violin
Head, String Division
University of Washington

"I have read with extreme interest Victor Pomer's important essay Preventing Physical Problems in Violin Playing.

I firmly believe this work to be among the most useful ones published in recent times. I will adopt it as a valuable source of consultation, and recommend it highly to colleagues and students."

Franco Gulli
Distinguished Professor of Music
School of Music
Indiana University

ISBN 0-9693449-0-2

Acknowledgements

I would like to acknowledge the kind assistance of Leo Siciliano, who has worked extensively on the text of this book, and offered many violinistic suggestions in clarifying and elaborating the material it presents.

I would also like to express my sincere thanks to Marnie Pomeroy for her many hours spent in helping to prepare this text. She has been equally generous in attending to numerous editorial matters connected with it.

Many thanks are due as well to Claire Heistek for her expertise in guiding and coordinating various phases of publication. To Frank Roseman and to my colleagues in the National Arts Centre Orchestra go warm thanks for their encouragement.

*C*ontents

Part III: THE LEFT HAND

Part IV: THE VIBRATO

Part V: CLOSING

*I*llustrations

Photos by F.R. Leclair, Ottawa.
Design by Le Phan,
Media Production Services,
University of Ottawa

*P*reface

I have dedicated this manual to the many hard-working violin/viola teachers who give so much time and personal attention to their students. Although their contribution to our communities goes largely unnoticed, these teachers establish the foundation for our students' development and shape the growth of each in a demanding vocation. Great benefit can result from the self-expression that they encourage.

One of a teacher's greatest responsibilities is to prevent physical discomfort in the student's playing, which may lead to strain and muscular injury. It is difficult to foresee, and beyond my purpose here to cover, the many specific problems caused by practicing incorrectly or with tensed muscles. Nevertheless, a problem identified can often be traced to the source and solved with some thought and adjustment.

This manual is not meant to be a Method. It proposes a few tested and proven suggestions which I consider important, and which I hope will guide the teacher in helping students perform with all possible ease.

Introduction

Choice of Instrument

The student should be equipped with a clear-sounding instrument along with a suitably balanced bow. Proper equipment affords more pleasure and encouragement to the young student and enhances progress. Before making a choice it may be necessary to test a few of the many commercial instruments and bows on the market, a fair number of which will be found both adequate and inexpensive. A well-fitting chinrest is important; the flatter models extending over the tailpiece are usually the best.

Part I

Posture

The Purpose of good posture is to allow the student to play without muscular strain. A relaxed body helps create a harmonious balance between player and instrument.

HOLDING THE VIOLIN

Rest the instrument on the collarbone in a horizontal position. Normally it should tilt slightly towards the right, without being overly slanted.

Imagine a line projecting straight out in front of the body from the left shoulder. The violin must point somewhat to the left of that line; it must not be pulled in front of the chest.

Keep the head straight; do not permit the left cheek to rest on the chinrest. The head, which has considerable weight of its own, should be held upright. Tilting it can result in strain and damage the neck muscles.

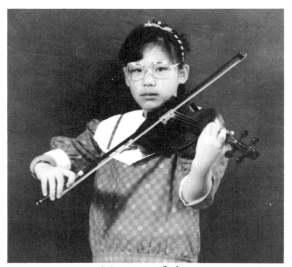
#1 Correct positioning of the Instrument

The chin sits just to the left of the tailpiece, where it is almost centered on the instrument. The cleft in the chin is approximately in line with the tailpiece.

The instrument is then held with the chin, shoulder, and hand, all working together in balance, with the hand exerting only slight pressure towards the body. (Although not appearing to do so, the fingers also press towards the body when in contact with the fingerboard.)

Shoulders should be kept low and even **at all times**. Allowances must be made, however, for individual builds. If the student has long arms, or low-set or sloping shoulders, the instrument should be held with the scroll slightly lower. A student with a very short neck is allowed to raise the shoulder a touch — but only imperceptibly.

Body weight should be distributed equally on both feet so that very little shifting is necessary. Walking around while practicing may relax some students, but it upsets balance. A correctly balanced body will often help prevent a sliding bow, and is fundamental in developing healthy playing habits and a secure technique.

THE VIOLIN IN RELATION TO THE LEFT ELBOW   (Refer to illustration #1 for correct violin - positioning)

For the player with an arm of average length, the left elbow will be approximately under the centre dividing line of the instrument. The elbow of a longer arm should be held somewhat left of centre. If the arm is short it may move towards the right, but never too far. This is the basic position for playing on the highest-pitched string. As a player crosses towards the lowest string, the elbow moves to the right. The wrist does not shift or move; the elbow takes both arm and wrist across in an even and flowing manner.

Beginning students should stay in first position until they are secure and comfortable with the functioning of the elbow.

A COMMON ERROR

Pushing the left elbow too far towards the right causes strain and tightening of muscles in the upper arm and shoulder. This affects the lower arm, which in turn results in stiff finger-action.

THE JAW AND NECK

A pronounced jaw or neck mark, which can become troublesome, is caused by excess movement of the instrument and rubbing between the jaw area and chinrest. Squeezing, as well, compounds these difficulties. The left side of the jaw or neck area can become very tender, and in many instances, an irritating lump may form that could require surgical removal. This problem is not easily recognized in the student's early years, but if observed, should be carefully examined by both teacher and student. The instrument should be stabilized, and unnecessary movement avoided.

Another fault which occasionally occurs in the jaw area, and which is difficult for the teacher to detect, is the clenching of teeth, indicating tension. In extreme cases, pain can develop under the left ear in the area of the back molars. If suspected, this clamping or pressing should be eliminated. A solution that I have found simple and effective is to have the student breathe through both nose and mouth while playing.

Part II
The Bow Arm

THE BOW GRIP

The style of grip described below is referred to as the «square» bow-hold. I favour this position because it permits the most natural and efficient use of the muscles of the hand, wrist, and arm.

The fingers are placed over the bow, with the fourth finger resting in a curled position on top of the stick. The first finger makes contact with the stick just before the second knuckle, which must not advance beyond (or over the top of) the stick. With the index and little finger positioned this way, the two middle fingers will fall relatively in place on the bow, the sensitive inner pads of the first joints making the correct contact.

Generally, the proper grip ensures that the thumb will settle across the centre of the longest finger. If the thumb is short, it should be moved towards or between the two middle fingers.

When the grip is correct, a relaxed open oval forms between the thumb and first finger. The formation of a crescent shape or narrow space would indicate that the first joint of the thumb has buckled inwards and upwards. This awkward position causes both thumb joints to stiffen and lock, and should be corrected within the next few lessons.

With guidance, the student will easily master the basics of the square-hand grip. As progress is made, the teacher should

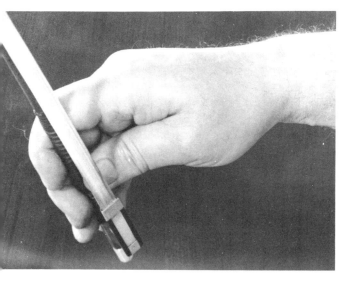

#2 A Locked Thumb (incorrect)

allow for the minor adjustments that the student, due to the size and structure of her/his hand, seems to favour and be comfortable with.

Of course, all schools of violin pedagogy that teach a particular bow-hold effectively, share this principle: the wrist must be held neither too high nor too low. Bowing-arm movement is not inhibited through a moderately positioned wrist, and weight is freely channeled to the hand and fingers.

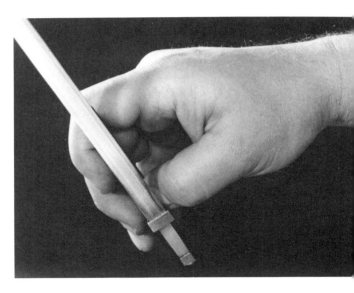

#3 A Relaxed Thumb (correct)

THE BOW ARM

The student, holding the bow correctly, places it on the violin A string without raising the shoulder. This relaxed lifting motion is performed with elbow remaining lower than shoulder. With the bow on the A string, the hand position adjusts so that the outer wrist-bone is slightly higher than, or almost in line with, the uppermost knuckle of the little finger.

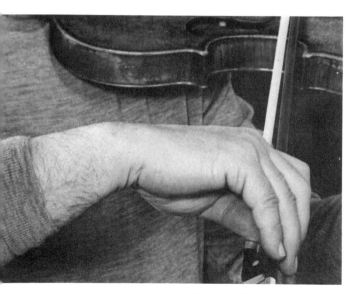

#4 Hand Position when Holding the Bow

Check for a proper grip and a low shoulder position. With the bow remaining on the A string, roll the wrist (**the arm will also roll**) slightly towards the left. If the little finger comes off the stick, the student has rolled too far.

This angled hand-position, coordinated with the arm while bowing, directs the bow in a straight line, equalizes down and up strokes, and helps control the balance of sound.

It is important to observe the structure of the student's arm. If the arm is of heavy build, the elbow may be set slightly lower to compensate. For the more slender arm, the elbow may be raised a little higher for the required weight and strength, but should not be lifted above the wrist-bone.

#5 Arm of Heavy Build

The arm is raised to its highest point when bowing on the lowest string, but it should not completely block out vision. The student ought to be able to see over the arm.

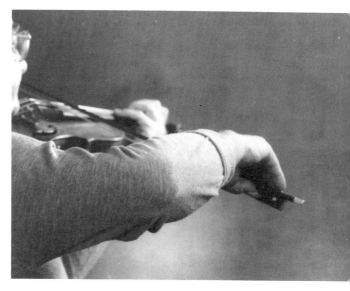

#6 Arm of Light Build

SUGGESTIONS FOR BEGINNING

For the first few lessons the student should play on the two middle strings only, using the central part of the bow. These easier and more natural balance points are best for the young player establishing a correct grip and bow stroke, while also becoming familiar with the sound and feel of the instrument.

When ready for a fuller use of the bow, the beginner will need guidance in keeping it straight at the end of the down stroke. The length of the bow stroke will, however, be limited by the length of the student's arm.

THE FULL AND EVEN BOW DRAW

As the arm, flexible and loose, draws the bow from frog to tip, a small roll to the left gradually occurs, involving the entire arm as one unit. Controlled weight is in this way directed to any part of the bow. The index or first finger is the lever of this controlled weight, and can supply, along with the rolling arm, any power required.

Note: *For the first few months, or until their muscles strengthen, young beginners should not press with the bow. Pressure applied too soon will result in clamping, or in an overly tight grip of the bow.*

THE WRIST-BREAK AND ARM REACH

An important element of the student's future bow draw is determined at this early stage of full-bow use. It is common for beginning students to «break» the wrist downwards before completing the full down-bow. The break is defined as a wrist joint collapsing and dropping below the level of the hand. This problem should be corrected without delay.

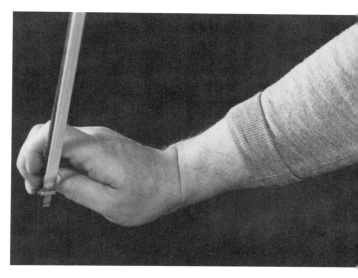

#7 Wrist Collapse

The student can now learn to extend, or reach out a little, while completing the fuller down-bow stroke. At the very end of the stroke, the wrist flexes more to the left or inner side rather than across the top.

The relatively short time needed to achieve this technique is well worth spending, as the student will now draw the bow in an uninterrupted straight line in the direction of the string vibration. Any rolling or rocking of the bow will also be eliminated.

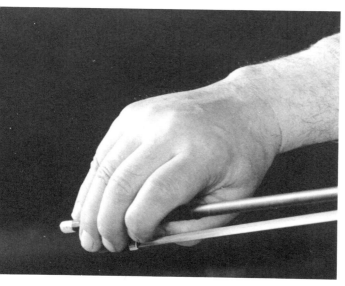

#8 Correct Position of the Wrist

Here is a simple exercise that combines both straight-line bowing and extended reach:

With the student squarely facing the music stand, place an object, such as a vase or lamp, about one metre (three to four feet) to the right of and thirty centimetres (one foot) forward from the student. The object is well within the student's vision. Now instruct the student to aim for the object on a long down-bow stroke. A correct draw is usually the result.

#9 Straight-Line Bowing and Extended Reach

31

Teachers need not be concerned about stiffness in the arm when bow direction is reversed at the tip. With the technique of the extended reach, a small loop forms naturally at the change of bow. I believe that early development of this linear sweep stroke will help prevent future physical difficulties, such as fatigue of the shoulder or elbow.

BOWING AND SOUND PRODUCTION

After the basic elements of bowing have been assimilated, gradually introduce the student to matters of sound production relating to:

- the various bow speeds;
- degrees of weight applied;
- placement of and effects produced by the different contact points of the bow between bridge and fingerboard.

Also explain and illustrate how to execute the many dynamics, and the various bow strokes with their effects. Begin with those performed on the string, such as a short martelé or staccato in the upper half of the bow.

When teaching the spiccato, do not present it as only a movement of the wrist. The arm participates in the spiccato stroke along with the wrist and fingers.

This is the ideal time to introduce the important role of the two middle fingers of the bow hand. For the spiccato and other off-the-string bowings, these two fingers — particularly the longer one — will have more to do. The fingers are still inclined in the direction of the bow stroke and string vibration, but the hand is less tilted. The inner pads of the first joints of these middle fingers are crucial in achieving the fine control and mastery of nuance that the advanced student will require.

The function of the little finger is to balance and stabilize the bow.

THE BOW CHANGE AT THE HEEL AND THE FLOATING SHOULDER

I was introduced to this technique while studying violin pedagogy at the Kiev Conservatory under Vadim K. Stetsenko. Mr. Stetsenko, the author of two highly regarded publications on the physics of string playing, assigned me the pleasant task of observing the bowing technique of the late David Oistrakh.

When asked to comment on my observations, I questioned my teacher as to how Oistrakh was able to sustain a long note or passage, especially when changing the bow at the heel, without any break in sound. Professor Stetsenko's immediate reply was «the floating shoulder», and he proceeded to explain.

The secret of this technique is to begin the down-bow with <u>exactly</u> the same finger and wrist position as the one which completes the up-bow. Once the connection of up-bow to down-bow has been made, the fingers and wrist may move freely.

A smooth change at the heel is accomplished by a low and relaxed shoulder riding or floating through the <u>final</u> instant of the bow connection, without movement of wrist or fingers.

This important stroke can be achieved within a few practice sessions, and will prove to be most valuable.

Supplement

Shoulder Supports

There is little doubt that a pad or cushion pressing on the bottom plate of an instrument will absorb sound and diminish volume. The comfort it provides, however, is worth some loss of tone. The shoulder rest helps the young student avoid raising the shoulder, and prevents ensuing tensions.

Advancing beyond the level of a beginner to a stage when full tone and sound are of greater importance, the student should choose a light-weight shoulder rest that does not come into contact with the body of the instrument. The type that attaches to the outer rim only will not noticeably affect the instrument's tone or volume.

An ideal shoulder rest of this kind, which is also adjustable, has been designed and marketed by Ottawa's Joseph Kun.

Shoulder supports are valuable to the professional orchestral musicians who spend many hours at a time in a set position. I would only caution against using a support that is too high or too thick, as this will decrease contact with the instrument and induce some players to pull the left shoulder slightly forward.

Part III

The Left Hand

WRIST POSITION

The left wrist is held in a straight, balanced, upright position natural to the individual. This will enable the fingers to feel the contact, the energy, and the strength of the hand beneath.

Some slight variation is acceptable, depending on finger length; but a laid-back or lazy hand positioning cannot be allowed. The fourth finger will not function properly if the wrist is not set straight.

#10 Laid-Back or Lazy Hand Positioning

THE LEFT THUMB

The thumb and the neck of the violin touch at a point either above or below the inner part of the thumb's first joint. Avoid deep-set positioning of the instrument at the base of the thumb where it meets the hand, as this hinders the vibrato.

Begin the student with the contact point just above the first joint. A space in the shape of a half oval, not unlike the oval of the bow hand, should form between the thumb and the hand. If there is no space, then the thumb joints have

#11 Balanced Upright Hand Positioning

tensed and are pressing inwards. This tension is also present if the first joint points or presses inwards. The thumb should be loose, rather than rigid or pressed tight against the neck. Correctly positioned, it will be in a fairly straight vertical line, and the bottom joint will be relaxed and able to pivot.

When the hand is shifting to or playing in the higher positions, the thumb should remain under the neck of the instrument.

#12 Deep-Set Positioning of the Instrument

#13 Tensed Thumb (incorrect)

#14 Relaxed Thumb (correct)

THE FINGERS OF THE LEFT HAND

A most important principle of left hand technique is that the finger should be ready to play on the spot where it is to fall. The quicker a passage is to be played, the closer the fingers should be to the string. Slow passages do not require preparation of the fingers except in string crossings. Unnecessary preparation may interfere with the vibrato.

Preparing the string-crossing finger in both upward and downward scale passages will help intonation and smoothness. Chords will also be handled more easily if the fingers are poised in place before they fall.

The preparing finger should not be tense, or it will affect the performing finger.

The habit of finger preparation will result in better memorization, control of intonation, speed, and quality of sound.

In both soft and loud passages, finger pressure should remain equal. If pressure is diminished in the soft passages and increased in the loud, intonation will vary.

Since all fingers are not of equal width and strength, the fourth finger must drop a little more firmly and from a slightly higher distance than the others. The fall of a finger originates at the bottom joint.

The tips of the fingers sometimes develop a leathery look and feel, not uncommon even among our most accomplished players. If hard callouses appear, too much finger pressure is being used. This is also the case if a mark on the neck becomes conspicuous.

There are three basic finger movements in violin/viola playing:

<u>Falling</u>: A controlled fall is neither uniformly fast nor abrupt. The movement begins at a measured speed and ends more quickly.

<u>Side</u>: This is the sideways movement of the finger up and down the string, such as in chromatic passages or slides. Pressure or weight is not exerted while the finger is in motion.

<u>Across</u>: When the finger moves across to another string, as in playing a fifth, pressure is lessened.

THE POSITIONS

The positions should be taught in order <u>or</u> combined in sequence when introduced to beginning players. For instance, the second position is presented before, or along with, the third — and so on. The common practice of skipping to third position after first does not have proven merit. On the contrary, a psychological set-back can be instilled in the student, who may come to regard the second and fourth positions as being 'hard'. If the positions are approached in their natural order as a routine procedure, the pupil will accept them as such.

SHIFTING OR CHANGE OF POSITION

Introduce shifting by having the student use the upper part of the arm to initiate the action. In this approach the thumb, which is held loosely at the neck of the instrument, travels along with the hand and arm as one unit.

I have found that students who begin with the arm shift develop assuredness and accuracy of movement. Those who begin with the leading wrist-and-hand method will often take considerably longer to attain correct movement, speed, and accuracy.

Only after this arm movement has become fluid should you teach the upward shift as lead by the wrist, and the downward, lead by the hand.

THE ARM SHIFT

With the student holding the instrument loosely in playing position, place your hand on his/her upper arm barely above the crease in the elbow, and slowly push towards the body. This action is quite relaxed and easy. Slowly repeat it with the student shifting into the first three or four positions.

#15 The Arm Shift

Guiding this arm motion from the beginning will facilitate later shifting into the upper register. As the hand passes fourth position, the arm starts its gradual smooth rotation to the right. When more adept at changing positions, the student must take care not to lessen the weight of the bow while shifting or sliding the finger.

Excessive use of glissando in the beginning stages of shift training is permissable for achieving the proper action, and for arriving at the correct note. The student's ear will soon adjust the fingers to a properly paced slide.

Part IV

The Vibrato

THE VIBRATO

A controversial subject! Can the vibrato be taught? What kind is most effective — wrist, finger, or arm?

In the average vibrato there is some combination of all **three** movements. Rarely is one generated by arm, wrist, or finger alone. The individual's favoured vibrato will, however, be noticed on longer notes — particularly the more obvious «arm» vibrato. Most players prefer an action predominantly from the wrist for smoothness and fuller control.

To achieve a good vibrato, the first joints of the fingers must develop strength and elasticity. An excellent way to help them do this is to practice shifting exercises along with chromatic scales, both in a gliding and staccato finger movement.

It is not wise to rush a student into using vibrato. A solid foundation of relaxed playing, based on the natural use of the muscles, should first be established. Once the correct basic training procedures have been implemented, many students will develop a vibrato on their own.

INTRODUCING THE STUDENT TO THE WRIST-FINGER VIBRATO

See that the student's left arm is held in correct playing position: perpendicular to the instrument, with the wrist straight, and the fingers poised over the fingerboard.

The second finger is placed on the A string (Viola D) in first position. Now guide the finger in making a light-touch <u>rolling</u> action directed towards the left shoulder. With this action clearly understood, and with fingers still poised over the fingerboard, the student now <u>rolls</u> the second finger slightly above and below the note for one slow, full down-bow.

When the rolling action is tried without the instrument, it is easy to do; but with the instrument, most students will need you to assist them in making the proper movement. On the fingerboard, their first tendency is to bend the wrist in and out, while at the same time keeping the finger stationary.

Once the correct movement has been mastered, extend this continuous slow vibrato practice by adding a full up-bow. For ease of balance, the student keeps using the second finger while gradually moving it onto the other strings.

Carefully monitor this beginning finger action, as it is the foundation for all further vibrato development.

When the continuous two-bow roll becomes comfortable, it is doubled to four full bows with (no bump) **smooth** bow changes.

Progress becomes quicker after this initial phase with the second finger. Repeat the same procedure with the third finger, then with a combination of the second and third fingers. The fourth finger is added in combination before going on to the first. The reason for this particular sequence is to have the hand set and turned correctly, so that when the first finger is finally applied, the hand does not open up and turn from the fingerboard.

Now we are on our way! Take two or three weeks to narrow, refine, and very slightly quicken the pace of the roll. Above all, have patience while the young muscles adapt to their new skill.

THE PULSE VIBRATO

This exercise will begin to develop vibrato control and to accustom the student to a more rapid finger motion, while strengthening the first joints.

Start with four beats per bow and with four shakes of the finger per beat. The **first** complete oscillation of each beat will be accented with a rapid kicking action of the finger.

Example:

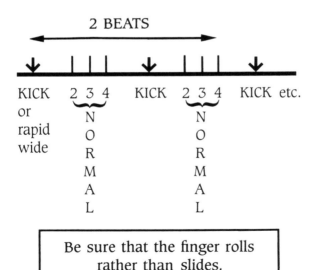

Be sure that the finger rolls rather than slides.

After the pulse vibrato has been assimilated, the following variations should be applied:

- two consecutive bows of four beats each
- four consecutive bows of four beats each
- strokes of six, eight, and ten beats

Apply various rhythms to the above, such as:

KICK 2 3 4 5 etc. KICK 2 3 etc. KICK 2 etc.

The longer rhythms will have fewer beats per bow, shorter rhythms more beats per bow.

Examples:

Kick 2 3 4 5 would be practiced with four to six beats per bow (any number of consecutive bows).

Kick 2 3 would be practiced with six to ten beats per bow (any number of consecutive bows).

When the preceding combinations of beats and rhythms can be performed comfortably by the student, spend two to three weeks working with different vibrato speeds.

51

FURTHER DEVELOPMENT OF THE VIBRATO

Surprisingly, only three to four months of work are needed for the vibrato to develop with the student's own individuality intact. Now it is time for the instructor to explain the effects, functions, and use of this ornament in playing.

Points to be understood:
- the vibrato must not affect the exact pitch of a note;
- regular and equal oscillations produce an even sound;
- no inflexible rules can be made about using the vibrato, but on low notes it is often slower and wider — on high notes, quicker and more concentrated;
- not every note has to be vibrated. An artistic use of the vibrato requires that it be varied according to the style and character of the composition, as well as according to the taste and imagination of the individual performer.

Note: *Should you find the student developing an excessively wide motion that changes the pitch of the note, discontinue the use of vibrato for a while to re-establish exact pitch. See that the thumb or fingers are not applying too much pressure.*

ARM VIBRATO

Some beginners will have difficulty in developing a wrist-finger vibrato because their fingers or wrists are not supple enough.

If this is the case, the student can try the arm-type vibrato, applying to it the wrist-finger exercises. If cultivated, a well-structured arm movement can become instinctive, with a certain lightness and freedom of action. Many violists and violinists prefer this vibrato to the wrist type, as the oscillations tend to be less rapid.

Make sure that the hand or arm is not held at too much of an angle, as an overly wide and less controlled movement will result. Violists with slim fingers or conical finger tips may angle enough so as to cover the string sufficiently with the finger pads.

Note that the shoulder should not play too active a part in the arm movement.

● ● ●

To conclude, stimulate your pupils into listening to music often, so that their inner voice or ear can discover the sound which most appeals to them and is compatible with their personalities. Help them to achieve this sound — one which they themselves animate from within.

#16 The Left Arm at Too-Angled a Position

#17 Correct Positioning of the Left Arm

54

Part V

Closing

SUMMARY

Periodic observation of the student's physical approach to the instrument should include the following:

1. POSTURE. Check for a balanced posture of the whole body. Do not neglect the positioning of the feet.
2. LEFT HAND. See that the left-hand position is straight, with the palm away from the neck of the instrument.
3. JAW AND NECK AREA. Correct immediately any clenching of teeth, also any clamping or any excessive movement of/on the instrument.
4. SHOULDERS. A low and relaxed position is essential. The shoulders should neither be raised to any extent, nor pulled forward to form a rounded back.
5. BOW CHANGES. Prevent constant snapping or flicking at the bow ends, which will destroy a smooth connection.

6. **BOW SPEED**. Speeding up when playing through the centre portion of the bow changes and distorts the sound.
7. **MANIPULATION OF THE BOW**. Slapping or dropping onto the strings with the bow produces a coarse attack. Don't, unless you require the effect.

ON PRACTICING

Good working habits are to be fostered at an early stage. The student should be prepared to make efficient use of the practice period. Careful, correct, and regular study is essential to progress. It must be emphasized that regular daily practice conditions the working muscles more effectively, and is generally more productive, than neglecting the instrument one day and overworking the next.

Senior students and professionals often do themselves considerable physical harm by overworking their muscles with three to four weeks of heavy practice when preparing for auditions or competitions. Although there may be events that require this kind of «cramming», it can usually be avoided by keeping in good playing condition, and by beginning to prepare earlier for performance.

PLAYING WHILE SITTING

Sitting upright is recommended because the body must be balanced. The spine should neither recline against the back of the chair nor should the shoulders hunch forward.

According to custom the feet are to be placed firmly on the floor, not crossed or tucked under the chair. The left foot is forward and the right foot back.

When playing in public the above foot positioning ought to be adhered to; but during the numerous rehearsals of the orchestral musician, I suggest putting the feet in any position that relaxes and gives relief to the player.

CLOSING COMMENTS FOR THE SENIOR PERFORMER

The adult string-player can easily overlook the importance of keeping physically fit. Young students are by nature very active, but many career-orientated players begin curtailing healthy physical activity at a surprisingly early age.

Think of the repetitive hours you have spent, and will spend, with arms suspended in front of you; and think of the cellist, arms wrapped around the instrument, similarly constricted to motions made in front of the body. It is hardly cause for wonder if, around the age of twenty-seven or twenty-eight, a string player notices signs of physical discomfort and wear. The process of aging has begun to affect the natural resiliency of youth. Correct early training and an easy, natural use of the muscles in playing may delay, and even prevent, any physical stress. But why run the risk: keep your body in good tone!

The muscles of a string player need to expand. Keep active by getting involved in any non-body contact sport that you enjoy. Swimming is excellent. Treat chores such as the shoveling of snow and the raking of leaves as therapeutic. Do not pamper your hands as they, too, need strength.

Here is a simple exercise that works well for me: lift your arms in front of you to shoulder level, then pull them back in a rowing movement, pressing and rotating towards the shoulder blades. Keep the head erect and the neck relaxed.

Well-tuned bodies will provide us with the physical and psychological balance required for long and successful careers.

About the Author

Victor Pomer (Pomeranski) was born in 1930 in Winnipeg, Manitoba. For the first twenty years of his career, he was involved in the many musical and educational activities of his native city. His sister Anne, a highly respected violin teacher, made a great and memorable contribution to the musical life of Winnipeg.

The Canada Council awarded Pomer a scholarship which enabled him to study the method of Russian String Pedagogy at the Kiev Conservatory from November 1959 to January 1961. As of 1988, he has been teaching for thirty-five years: privately, at summer camps, at the University of Manitoba, and currently, at the University of Ottawa.

The fall of 1988 marks his fortieth year as a performing orchestral violinist, and his twentieth with the National Arts Centre Orchestra, of which he is a founding member.

His two sons are both accomplished musicians. Scott, a violist, and Shaun, a cellist, at present are attending the School of Music at Indiana University.

NOTES